Don·Bousquet's
NEW ENGLAND

Don·Bousquet's
NEW ENGLAND

Cartoons from the pages of *YANKEE* Magazine

YANKEE BOOKS

A division of Yankee Publishing Incorporated,
which also publishes *Yankee* Magazine and
The Old Farmer's Almanac.

Designed by Margo Letourneau

Most of the cartoons in this collection
have previously appeared in *Yankee* Magazine.

Yankee Publishing Incorporated
Dublin, New Hampshire 03444

First Edition
First Printing, 1989
Copyright 1989 by Yankee Publishing Incorporated

SKU 01

ISBN: 0-89909-167-9

BOB, LIVING A HERETOFORE QUIET
LIFE IN NASHUA, N.H., IS SLOWLY
DRIVEN INSANE BY THE LAST
LEAF OF FALL.

"DID IT EVER OCCUR TO YOU, MARGARET, THAT YOU HAVE AN UNNATURAL FEAR OF EMPTY-NEST SYNDROME?"

"SOME DUDE CALLED ROGER WILLIAMS WANTS TO BUY SOME LAND AND SET UP A SOCIETY BASED ON RELIGIOUS FREEDOM AND DISCOUNT DEPARTMENT STORES."

"I'M STANDING HERE WITH OLGA HOOGASIAN OF PRESQUE ISLE, THE VERY FIRST FEMALE C.P.A. OF ARMENIAN EXTRACTION SCHEDULED TO FLY ABOARD AMERICA'S SPACE SHUTTLE."

SECRET BOVINE STRAIN BRED IN
THE WILDS OF VERMONT
... THE PIT COW.

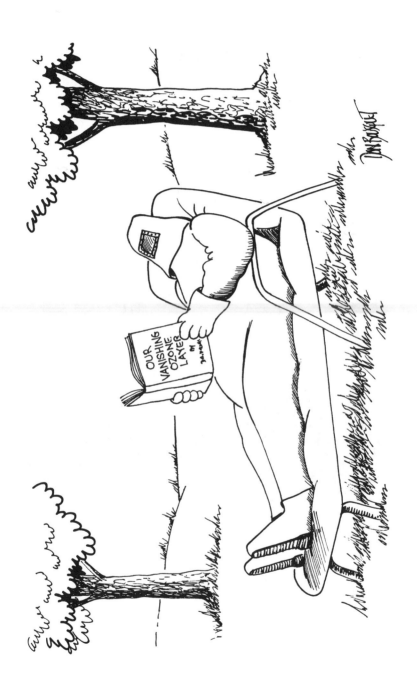

"HI, MR. PIERCE, WELCOME BACK...
HEY, IT WASN'T YOUR APPENDIX
AFTER ALL..."

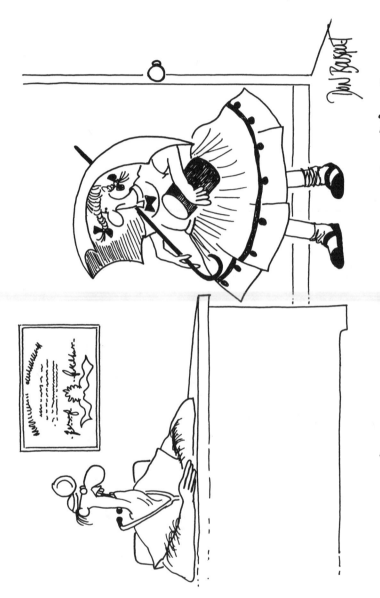

BEFORE HE CHANGED HIS NAME AND MOVED OUT WEST, WYATT TWERP USED TO HANG OUT WITH THE BOYS AT THE LONG BRANCH SALOON IN BURLINGTON, VERMONT.

THERE ARE STILL A FEW NEW
ENGLAND INDUSTRIES THAT CAN'T
HACK A TRANSITION TO THE SUN BELT.

WHISTLER'S BROTHER-IN-LAW

USS OLD STURBRIDGE VILLAGE

... THE NAVY'S OLDEST NUCLEAR SUB.

"OKAY, WHO'S GOT THE SEAFOOD PLATTER FLAMBE'?"

IMPROVING CONDITIONS IN THE BASEMENT OF THE REGISTRY OF MOTOR VEHICLES

"OKAY, SO THAT'S A HALF-DOZEN FISH HEADS AN' A SIDE ORDER OF RAW EELS...YOU WANT COFFEE, OR WHAT?"

EVEN IN SEVENTEENTH CENTURY SALEM, WIND SHEAR WAS A SERIOUS PROBLEM.

" EXCUSE ME, BUT I COULDN'T HELP BUT NOTICE THAT YOU PUT VINEGAR ON YOUR FRENCH FRIES AND THAT YOU'RE WEARING BROWN SOCKS WITH BLACK SHOES. WHAT PART OF RHODE ISLAND DO YOU COME FROM ? "

FRANCHISED BED AND BREAKFAST

SLIPPERY PILING

THE BETTER NEW ENGLAND HOTELS
OFFER COMPLIMENTARY BREAKFASTS.

DIE-HARD NEW ENGLANDERS IN FLORIDA

" HOW ABOUT WE TURN THE AIR CONDITIONING DOWN TO FORTY-FIVE AND CRANK UP THE OL' WOOD STOVE ?! "

"OF COURSE, YOU COULD SEEK A SECOND OPINION, BUT GOOD LUCK FINDING ANOTHER ORTHOPEDIC SURGEON IN THIS HICK TOWN WITH A DEGREE FROM HARVARD MEDICAL SCHOOL AND THE KEYS TO A LATE-MODEL MERCEDES WITH A LEATHER INTERIOR."

ON THE NEXT EPISODE OF
BANGOR VICE...

" OK, PUNK, WE'RE BOOKIN' YOU ON A 714...THAT'S TRANSPORTING LAWN ORNAMENTS ACROSS A COUNTY LINE FOR IMMORAL PURPOSES."

GROWING UP IN NEW ENGLAND: THE DIFFICULT YEARS

RECOILING IN HORROR AND DISBELIEF, DEBORAH DISCOVERS THAT SOMEONE OR <u>SOMETHING</u> HAS LEFT DUBLIN, NEW HAMPSHIRE, OFF HER FIFTH GRADE CLASSROOM GLOBE!

RECENTLY THE OLD STURBRIDGE
VILLAGE PLAYBOY CLUB CLOSED
ITS DOORS FOR GOOD.

"...AND WE COULD NOT HAVE SURVIVED THAT FIRST WINTER WITHOUT OUR FRIENDS THE NARRAGANSETTS AND THEIR RECIPE FOR FETTUCINE ALFREDO..."

HARD CORE BIRD WATCHER

MAINE JUVENILE DELINQUENT

" LOBSTERS DOWN ANOTHER TWO AND ONE-EIGHTH... LOOKS LIKE WE SIT ON THESE BABIES AT LEAST ANOTHER WEEK."

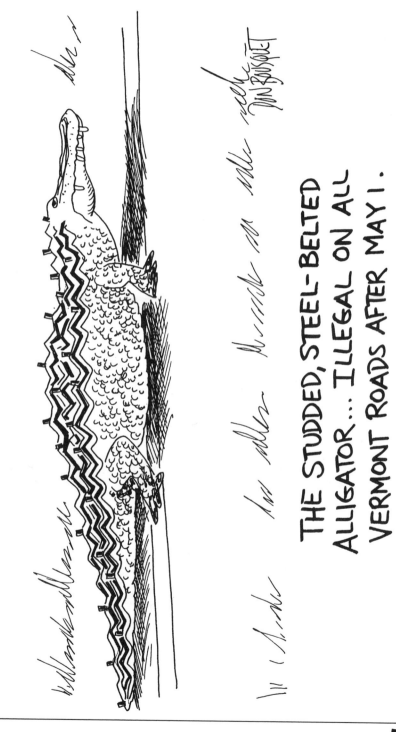

THE STUDDED, STEEL-BELTED ALLIGATOR... ILLEGAL ON ALL VERMONT ROADS AFTER MAY 1.

" HOW DO I KNOW YOU'RE THE REAL
TOOTH FAIRY AND NOT JUST SOME
DUDE WITH A MOLAR FETISH ? "

"HEY, LADY... WE STILL IN THE WHITE MOUNTAIN NATIONAL FOREST?"

" NO, THEY DON'T SEEM TO BE PURPLE MARTINS... "

" You WANT FRIES WITH THAT ? "

BRILLIANT AS HE WAS, YOUNG
BEN FRANKLIN NEVER DID PERFECT
THE 'FRANKLIN HASSOCK'...

" EXTRA! READ ALL ABOUT IT!!
FOLIAGE SEASON ENDS UP NORTH...
THOUSANDS FLEE VERMONT AND NEW HAMPSHIRE
AND RETURN TO MIAMI! "

" SHE RUNS A BED AND BREAKFAST IN MANCHESTER... BREAKFAST IS OPTIONAL."

"GOOD LORD! MARGARET, LOOK AT THIS... DUMP STICKERS ARE GOING UP ANOTHER TWO DOLLARS!!"

♪ "SLEEP TIGHT, DON'T LET THE
BED BUGS BITE." ♪♪

" YOU'RE ON A LIQUID DIET FOR NOW, MR. WILSON, BUT YOU CAN HAVE AS MUCH AS YOU WANT. "

" TOOK HIM OUT OF THE WOOD RIVER
DOWN IN HOPE VALLEY, SPRING OF '35...
BUT THEY DON'T MAKE NO REAL
TROUT NO MORE ! "

"WELL, EVERYTHING SEEMS TO BE IN ORDER... JUST AS WE LEFT IT IN THE FALL."

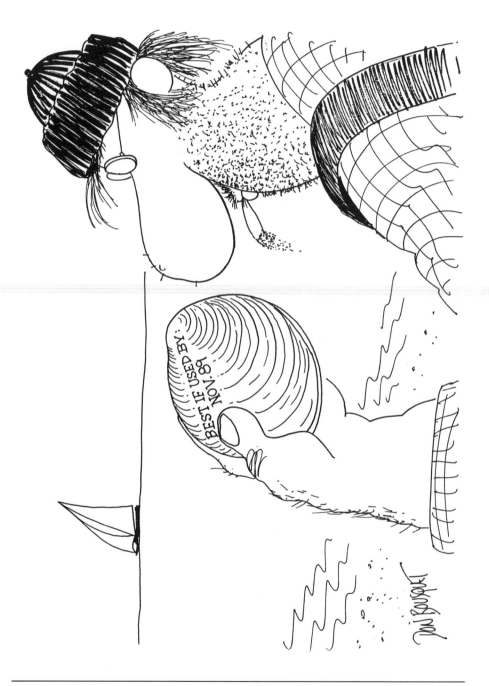

" HOW'S THE INDIAN PUDDING TODAY? "

" BILLY ZIMMERMAN, YOU GET DOWN HERE
THIS MINUTE ! IF YOU'RE TOO SICK FOR SCHOOL
YOU'RE TOO SICK TO GO OUT AND PLAY !! "

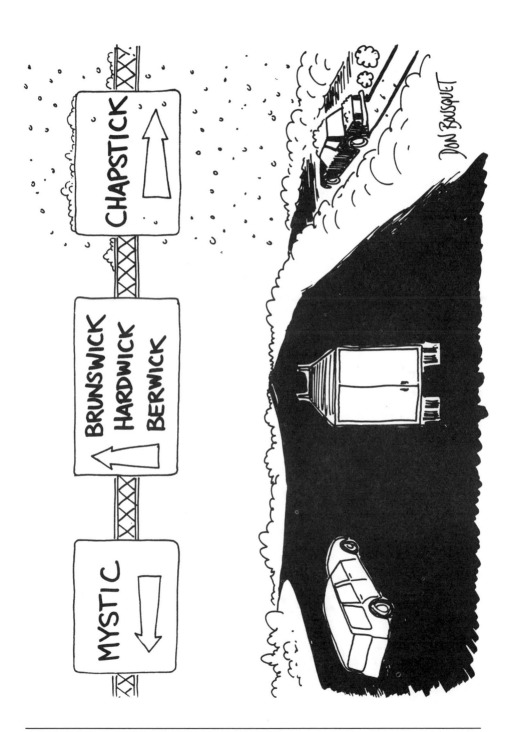

FAST FOOD FAILURE AT FENWAY PARK:
BOSTON BAKED BEANS ON A BUN.

MASSACHUSETTS ISLANDS

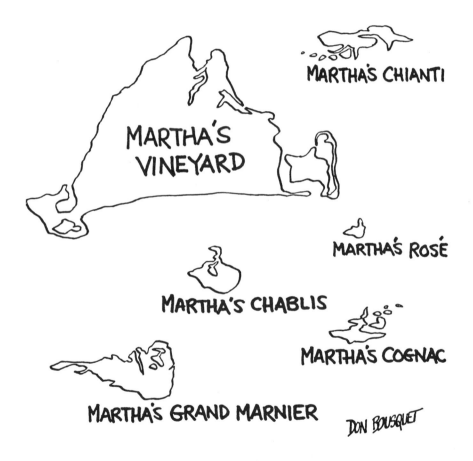

MARTHA'S CHIANTI

MARTHA'S VINEYARD

MARTHA'S ROSÉ

MARTHA'S CHABLIS

MARTHA'S COGNAC

MARTHA'S GRAND MARNIER

DON BOUSQUET

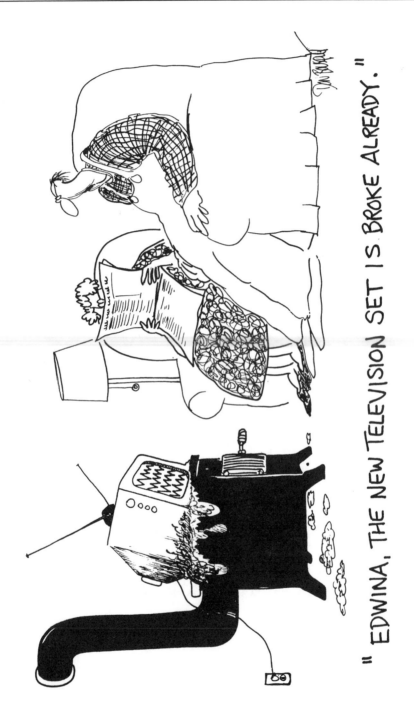

"Edwina, the new television set is broke already."

"I'M LOST IN A STORM ABOUT TWELVE MILES NORTH OF BARRE ON SOME RINKY-DINK ROAD OFF ROUTE 2 — BUT, YOU KNOW THE CRAZIEST THING?... THE PHONE BOOTH HAS ALL THESE DISCARDED PIECES OF CLOTHING AROUND IT AND...HELLO?...HELLO?..."

YUPPIE PIRATE

" TWO HUNDRED AND FORTY POUNDS...
NEXT TIME, TRY DROPPING THE BRIEFCASE
BEFORE GETTING ON THE SCALE, BUTTERBALL."

" OOOOO, FRANCINE! I'M JUST SO
HELPLESS AROUND MEN WITH SUCH
BIG MUSSELS! "

About the Author

Don Bousquet was born in Pawtucket, Rhode Island, on St. Patrick's Day, 1948. He was raised in Richmond, Rhode Island, and graduated from Chariho High School. Before attending the University of Rhode Island, where he majored in anthropology, Don served in the Navy as a photographer and worked as a private investigator for the Pinkerton Detective Agency.

His cartoons regularly appear in several New England newspapers, as well as in *Yankee* Magazine, *The Old Farmer's Almanac,* and all over Rhode Island in various advertising and commercial ventures. Don lives in Narragansett, Rhode Island, with his wife, Laura, and his two sons, Nathan and Michael. His hobbies include restoring antique cars, boating, and sailplanes.

Photograph by Sallie Wharton Latimer